Pastor Nick & Becky

GOD'S PROMISE

OF

HEALING

Paula A. Struble

By Rev. Paula A. Struble

Ps. 25:14

"Scripture quotations taken from The Amplified Bible, Copyright 1954, 1958, 1962, 1964, 1965, 1987 by The Lockman Foundation. All rights reserved. Used by permission. (www.Lockman.org)"

© 2012 Rev. Paula A. Struble
All Rights Reserved.

No part of this publication may be reproduced, stored in a retrieval system, or transmitted, in any form or by any means, electronic, mechanical, photocopying, recording, or otherwise, without the written permission of the author.

First published by Dog Ear Publishing
4010 W. 86th Street, Ste H
Indianapolis, IN 46268
www.dogearpublishing.net

ISBN: 978-1-4575-0940-7

This book is printed on acid-free paper.

Printed in the United States of America

CONTENTS

Chapter 1	Redemptive Revelation 1
Chapter 2	Is God's healing for everyone? .. 9
Chapter 3	What Is Faith? 21
Chapter 4	Faith and Patience Inherits the Promises of God 32
Chapter 5	Faith Without Works is Dead 38
Chapter 6	Fear, Doubt and Unbelief 46
Chapter 7	Hold Fast To Your Confession Of Faith 56
Chapter 8	Hindrances To Your Promise .. 67
Chapter 9	Do You Know Who You Are In Christ? 79
Chapter 10	What Do You Think? 86

PREFACE

I believe that as you read this book and meditate on the words contained in this book, God will grant you revelation knowledge into the truths of His Word regarding His promise to heal.

This book may seem controversial to some, but to others the light will come on.

"And He (Jesus) replied to them, "To you it has been given to know the secrets and mysteries of the kingdom of heaven, but to them it has not been given." For whoever has spiritual knowledge, more will be given, and he will be furnished richly so that he will have abundance; but to those who have not, even what he has will be taken away." (Matthew 13:11-12)

I also believe that some will be healed while they are reading this book; while others will have their faith increased to walk out their healing and see the manifestation. Yes, and there will be those who will develop their faith to know and understand that they never have to be sick another day in their lives.

ACKNOWLEDGEMENTS

I would like to begin first and foremost by acknowledging and giving thanks to the Holy Spirit of God for helping me to write this book. Now I really understand how the Bible was God-breathed (given by His inspiration) to the apostles.

A special thanks to Pastor Chuck Kennedy of Faith International Christian Center in Bradenton, Florida. I sat under his teaching for several years and it changed my life. Thank you Pastor Chuck, for your faithfulness and steadfastness.

I also want to thank my husband, Don for his encouragement and help in editing this book. I am very blessed to have a husband like him. He seems to always find time to help me even with his busy schedule as Senior Pastor and CEO of the National Christian Conservative Church ministerial fellowship in Lakewood Ranch, Florida.

Also, I give credit to Corrie Kyle for editing this book. Corrie is an awesome first grade teacher who presently resides in Port Charlotte, Florida with her 15 year old son. She also was healed of Lyme disease a few years ago. She informed me that she no longer catches classroom sicknesses since she has applied what she learned from this book.

CHAPTER 1

REDEMPTIVE REVELATION

*H*appy (blessed, fortunate, enviable) is he who has the God of (special revelation) Jacob for his help, whose hope is in the Lord his God. (*Psalm 146:5*)

Many people in the body of Christ love the Lord and are Spirit-filled, but are going home before their time, with all kinds of sickness and disease. They are not living the life of wholeness that God intended, because of the lack of *Redemptive Revelation*. They do not have the revelation of what Christ has already done for them on the cross.

Where there is no vision (Redemptive Revelation) of God, the people perish.
(Proverbs 29:18)

The word vision in Hebrew is Chazown which means a sight (mentally), i.e., dream, revelation, oracle or vision. Also, Chazah means to gaze at, or to mentally perceive, contemplate, have a vision of, behold, look or see.

Redemption in Greek means: the act, ransom in full, riddance, salvation, deliverance and redemption through His blood.

Christ purchased our freedom (to ransom, to redeem, to atone for) of those who were subject to the law, that we might be adopted and have sonship conferred upon us and be recognized as God's sons. (*Galatians 4:5, 6*)

We really know that we are his sons and daughters because verse 6 says that God sent the Holy Spirit into our hearts crying "Abba Father" to confirm that. We are no longer slaves, but sons, daughters and heirs through Christ. He bought and paid for us with his blood.

Christ purchased our freedom, redeeming us from the curse (doom) of the Law and its condemnation. He became a curse for us. For it is written, cursed is everyone who hangs on a tree (is crucified). (*Galatians 3:13*)

Whom the Lord sets free is free indeed.

Praise the Lord! For the Law of the Spirit of life, which is in Christ Jesus (the Law of my new being) has freed me from the Law of sin and death; sickness, disease, death, decay, destruction, lack, poverty, misery, fear, and corruption. (*Romans 8:2*)

I am not subject to the old Law anymore, as long as I live and walk after the dictates of the Spirit and not the dictates of the flesh. That tells me that the old Law is still in effect according to *Romans 8:1*. It is just like the Law of gravity. Don't try jumping off of a building, because the Law of gravity is still in effect, even if you can't see it.

There are many people in the world today that are still living under the old Law reaping sin, death, sickness, disease, decay, fear destruction, lack, poverty and misery. If we walk, and are led by the Spirit of God, we will not fulfill the desires of the flesh.

Christ freed me from the old Law.

God's children can still reap those things from the old Law if they do not conform their minds and thinking to agree with God and be led by His Spirit.

We must be in agreement with God and His Word, and be led by the Holy Spirit that dwells in us.

> *Do not be conformed to this world (this age), fashioned after and adapted to its external, superficial customs, but be transformed (changed) by the entire renewal of your mind.*
>
> **(Romans 12:2)**

The Law of the Spirit of life, liberty and freedom contains our Promise of healing and divine health. We are heirs to these great and precious promises.

The word Revelation in the Greek means: disclosure, appearing, coming, to lighten, manifestation, be revealed, revelation; to take off the cover, uncovering the veil of darkness. It is the communication of the knowledge of God to the soul.

It reveals the hidden things; insight into mysteries and secrets.

A very good example of *Redemptive Revelation* is in *Matthew 16:13-17*. Jesus said to them (disciples), "But who do you yourselves say that I am?" Peter replied, "You are the Christ, Son of the Living God."

In verse 17, Jesus answered him, "Blessed are you Simon Bar-Jonah, for flesh and blood (men) have not revealed this to you, but my Father who is in heaven."

He goes on to say, in Verse 18, that His church will be built on the Revelation Knowledge of who Christ is and what he provided and accomplished at the cross for us (church). The church is not built on Peter. It is built on the Revelation of the Christ and His finished work.

God can give you revelation through dreams and visions.

Some years ago, I competed in figure skating events and I now use these illustrations several times in my book. When I was learning my axle (an axle is a 1½ revolution jump), I fell and pulled the ligaments in my shoulder. It was extremely painful. I said in my heart that I would not continue to practice that jump any longer.

That night, God spoke to me in a dream. (Pastors are symbolic for God in dreams and visions.) My pastor had his hand on the back of my shoulder.

He gently pushed me forward. When I woke up in the morning, my shoulder was completely healed and I heard the Holy Spirit say, "Go forward."

I went to the ice rink that day and continued practicing my axle and got it that day. Praise the Lord!

Things are hidden temporarily only as a means to revelation. For there is nothing hidden except to be revealed, nor is anything temporarily kept secret except in order that it may be made known. *(Mark 4:22)*

Let's go back again to the word Redemption (salvation). Salvation, in the Greek, is Soteria which means: deliverance, set free, rescue, preservation, safety, healing, protect, do well, to be (make) whole, and sound mind. Also the word Salvation in *Psalm 91* means get the victory and prosperity. Awesome!

This tells me that when I accepted Christ as my Lord and Savior, my Redemption (salvation) included divine health and healing.

Wow! I don't have to be sick and diseased anymore.

If we look at *Matthew 8:17*, it tells us that He fulfilled what was spoken by the prophet Isaiah. He, Himself, took (in order to carry away) our weaknesses and infirmities and bore away our diseases.

The word infirmities in Greek (Astheneia), means feebleness of body or mind, malady, frailty, disease, infirmity, sickness and weakness.

So, if He took (past tense) and carried them away, then why are we carrying them? If He already bore away our diseases, then why are we bearing them?

Also, in *1 Peter 2:24*, "By His wounds you have been healed." Notice that it was already done, past tense.

Another favorite scripture is *Isaiah 53:4-5*. Surely He has borne (past tense) our grief (sicknesses, weaknesses, and distresses) and carried (past tense) our sorrows and pains of punishment, yet we ignorantly considered Him stricken, smitten, and afflicted by God (as if with leprosy).

But He was wounded (past tense) for our transgressions, He was bruised (past tense) for our guilt and iniquities; the chastisement needful to obtain peace and well-being for us was upon Him, and with the stripes that wounded Him, we are healed and made whole.

Personally, I have been healed of many things over the years simply by speaking the word "By His stripes I am healed."

But when something life-threatening came upon me back in 2003, I simply did not have the faith or the *Redemptive Revelation* to overcome it.

Something that is minor and not life threatening is one thing, but when it can take your life, it's another story altogether.

I was attacked with Graves disease back in 2003. Graves disease is an immune disorder that attacks the thyroid. The only cure is to have the thyroid removed and take drugs the rest of your life, or have the thyroid killed with radiation and take drugs the rest of your life. Not much of a choice.

My thyroid began running at a high speed, which caused my body to have tremors and shake all over. My ears would throb constantly. I began loosing weight and my muscles became very weak.

Ice skating was always a part of my life for many years. As my muscles became weak, I couldn't do the jumps that I loved doing for so long. Also, I couldn't put on my own makeup because my hands would shake too much.

I immediately sought out a doctor. As a matter of fact, I went to three different doctors and they all diagnosed Graves disease.

Deep inside, I wasn't willing to do what they prescribed, even though the symptoms were quite noticeable.

Thank you Lord for taking those 39 lashes for me.

CHAPTER 2

IS GOD'S HEALING FOR EVERYONE?

*T*herefore, since these (great) promises are ours, beloved, let us cleanse ourselves from everything that contaminates and defiles body and spirit, and bring our consecration to completeness in the reverential fear of God. *(2 Corinthians 7:1)*

For as many as are the promises of God, they all find their Yes (answer) in Him (Christ). For this reason we also utter the Amen (so be it) to God through Him to the glory of God. *(2 Corinthians 1:20)*

Therefore, inheriting the promise (healing) is the outcome of faith and depends entirely on our faith, in order that it might be given as an act of grace (unmerited favor), to make it stable and valid and guaranteed to all his (Abraham's) descendants. You are an heir to these promises through faith. *(Romans 4:16)*

Also, *2 Peter 1:4* tells us that, He has bestowed (already done, waiting to be manifested by your faith), on us His precious and exceedingly great promises, so that through them you may escape from the moral decay (rottenness and corruption) that is in the world and become sharers (partakers) of the divine (Theos) (god-like, supreme divinity, magistrate) nature of God. That is awesome! Meditate on that!

Wow! You, through the promises of God, share in God's divine nature. I guarantee you that He doesn't have sickness and disease, maladies, infirmities, feebleness and never has to get a flu shot!

So let us seize and hold fast and retain without wavering the hope we cherish and confess and our acknowledgement of it, for He who promised is reliable (sure) and faithful to His word. (*Hebrews 10:23*)

Healing and divine health are for all of God's people. If you are born again, ransomed by the blood of Jesus, then healing belongs to you. It is your covenant right and inheritance. Christ paid the price for all of his children, not just some.

The promise is obtained through faith.

You may say, "Well, my aunt was a powerful woman of faith and she died of cancer." I am very sorry to hear that, but it doesn't change the truth of God's word.

I met a man, who came to one of our meetings. He shared with us the terrible pain he had been enduring since he had back surgery and other things as well. He said that it was his cross to bear and that God was probably trying to teach him something.

During my testimony, the Holy Spirit quickened me to speak directly to him and tell him that because he was being so effective in his ministry, satan didn't like it, and that this was an all-out attack to destroy him and his ministry to hurting people. He was being oppressed by the devil.

Whose report will you believe?

When the devil attacked his back, he received the suggestion and had back surgery. Now he's in worse shape than before. That doesn't mean that he can't get back on the right track and stop believing the lies of the enemy.

Whose report will you believe? The report of the devil, or the report of the Lord?

Also, the enemy gets many people addicted to drugs (pain medication) after the surgery.

Satan will tell you that you need to see a doctor. It's probably something serious. "This could be the big one." Once you do that, he has a stronghold. Strongholds are made up of thoughts. Yes, the pain is real, yes it hurts, but it is a lying symptom.

It is never God's will for you to be sick or diseased!

I have been in the Worship Dance Ministry for many years. As I was practicing a special ministry dance, I turned my ankle slightly; nothing serious. I sat down and took authority over it. No problem! I finished the practice and felt ready to minister that Sunday.

Several hours later, my ankle became excruciatingly painful. I couldn't stand or put any pressure on my ankle. My husband had to carry me to bed. I took a couple of pain pills and sought the Lord. I knew I was to minister this dance that Sunday (three days away). I asked the Lord to show me what was going on?

The Lord spoke to me and said, "Do you think you are any different than my disciples? If you want to serve me, you will be attacked."

I went to sleep that night and when I awakened in the morning I took a step of faith, literally and stepped out of bed and started walking and putting pressure on my ankle. I decided I would go ice skating that day, and I did. What a great time I had.

You might be thinking; "Well, I tried that faith stuff and it didn't work. Maybe faith tried you.

The promise of divine health and healing are for all who will believe God's promise; be in agreement with His word, speak it and act upon it. God is faithful (reliable, trustworthy) and, therefore; ever true to His promise, and He can be depended upon. *(1 Corinthians 1:9)*

It's not always easy to believe God and walk by Faith when the symptoms and the doctors say just the opposite. But God's word tells us that without faith it is impossible to please God and that the just (you) shall live by faith. We walk by faith and not by sight.

We don't go by the circumstances, what we feel, or what we see.

My first mistake from the beginning was to believe those symptoms and start acting upon them. The devil now had a foothold (stronghold).

You might say, "What did the devil have to do with it?" Everything! The Word clearly tells us what oppression is and where it comes from.

Now Jesus was teaching in one of the synagogues on the Sabbath. There was a woman there who for eighteen years had an infirmity caused by a spirit (a demon of sickness). She was bent completely forward and utterly unable to straighten herself up or to look upward.

And when Jesus saw her, He called her to Himself and said to her "Woman, you are released from your infirmity!" Then He laid His hands on her, and instantly she was made straight, and she recognized and thanked and praised God." *(Luke 13:11-13)*

The reason the Son of God was made manifest (visible) was to undo (destroy, loosen, and dissolve) the works the devil has done.

(1 John 3:8)

I know there are many children of God that are held captive and in bondage to sex, drugs and alcohol. I loose, destroy, and dissolve those strongholds and chains over every one of them in Jesus name. These people are being oppressed by Satan.

Even if you have abused your body with substances like drugs, alcohol and nicotine for most of your life, healing is yours. That promise belongs to you no matter how bad it looks. I don't care if the doctor tells you that your liver is destroyed, or anything else.

Because, if you acknowledge and confess with your lips that Jesus is Lord and in your heart believe (trust and rely on the truth) that God raised Him from the dead, you will be saved. *(Romans 10:9)*

The word saved in the Greek is Sozo. It means safe; i.e., delivered, protected, healed, preserved, do well, be (make) whole. The devil was behind getting you addicted in the first place.

Let me make one thing clear. We need to take care of our temple of the Holy Spirit that God has put us in charge of. Treat it right, with proper rest and nutrition. You can't eat Twinkies for breakfast, lunch and dinner. God gave us every herb bearing seed and plant for good nutrition. *(1 Corinthians 6:19-20)*

Thank the Lord for doctors: God uses doctors, but it could be detrimental to your life to go to a doctor before you consult God. King Asa did this, and it cost him his life. He did not seek the Lord, but relied on the physicians. *(2 Chronicles 16:12, 13)*

You could end up worse off after surgery and develop worse problems than you had before. You could even end up dieing.

Some of those drugs that the doctor puts you on can end up killing you or causing worse problems. Always seek the Great Physician first! Remember, He lives within you.

Make your appointments with God every day.

You have an enemy who comes to kill, steal and destroy. Jesus came that we might have life (vitality) and have it more abundantly. (John 10:10)

What part of kill, steal and destroy don't you understand?

God anointed and consecrated Jesus of Nazareth with the Holy Spirit and with strength, ability and power. He went about doing good and, in particular, curing all who were harassed and OPPRESSED by the power of the devil, for God was with Him. *(Acts 10:38)*

Oppressed means to exercise dominion against, to enslave, to utterly bring into bondage, to hunt down, follow after, pronounce guilty, condemn, cause calamity, manifest, evident, to struggle against, subdue, overcome, to shame, to consume wholly (cancer), veil, cover, hide, to lie down (be sick), to break, find fault with and blame. Does that sound like the oppressor?

Satan is the oppressor. Oppression is sickness and disease, (proof positive). Need I say more? He was oppressing me with Graves disease. Be well balanced (temperate, sober of mind), be vigilant and cautious at all times; for that enemy of yours, the devil, roams around like a lion roaring in fierce hunger, seeking someone to seize upon and devour. *(1 Peter 5:8)*

If you are ever going to overcome that sickness or disease, you must understand and know your enemy. You cannot conquer the disease or sickness if you do not know where it comes from. You must know the strategy of the enemy or you will be defeated.

The word tells us to be subject to God. Resist the devil (stand firm against him) and he will flee from you.

(James 4:7)

John G. Lake wrote, "The reason people become sick is the same reason that they fall into sin. They surrender to the suggestion that the devil makes, and it takes possession of the heart."

Satan has you convinced that everybody gets that, or you must not be eating right, or God is trying to get your attention, or maybe you think it is your cross to bear.

You better get that flu shot, or you'll get the flu. Also, that pain seems pretty convincing. Sickness and *dis*-ease are just the same. There is no difference. The suggestion of oppression is presented, and becoming frightened, the disease, sickness or pain secures a foothold (stronghold). A stronghold is made up of thoughts.

The devil wants you to think his way. You get a pain or symptom and start thinking something is wrong, or this could be serious and then start speaking it, and then act upon it.

Know the strategies of your enemy.

I believed the lie of the devil when he suggested that I must not be eating right. Then, I spoke and acted upon his suggestion. Now, he had me.

I remember the first doctor that I went to. He actually told me that God gives sickness and disease and that Satan heals. Well, I set him straight, and I did not go back to him. There are a lot of foreign doctors out there with some strange beliefs.

The second doctor I went to see just confirmed the diagnosis of the first.

The third doctor that I went to see was in the Orlando area. He thought he could help me by putting me on the right supplements and also giving me a drug which regulated my Thyroid. I started to feel better almost immediately. The symptoms were gone.

Every month I would have blood tests done and drive to Orlando, Florida from Sarasota. This went on for two years.

In the meantime, I was being stirred to leave the church that I was in and go to a word of faith church. There were many people in my former church that were sick and some even died. I needed to hear the word of faith, build and develop my faith, to see the manifestation of my healing. My faith began to grow.

Faith is like a muscle. You have to exercise it to make it strong.

If you are ever to have the victory, you must be obedient to whatever the Holy Spirit tells you to do. Your faith cannot increase, and grow to overcome, by staying in your comfort zone. Sometimes you have to get out of the boat and go where you can hear the word of faith. It is spiritual nutrition.

The struggle (battle) was on and I needed to fight the good fight of faith. I had to fight to believe what God said over what the doctor and circumstances were saying. I believe the only battle we have to fight, is the battle to believe God over the circumstances.

Let me be clear. Don't stop taking your medication unless you have that revelation (Rhema) word from God. Then you need to be obedient. Other than that, don't do it, because the devil knows if <u>you</u> really know, and he will take you out. You will understand this more as I continue sharing my testimony.

Fight the good fight of faith.

CHAPTER 3

WHAT IS FAITH?

Now Faith is the assurance (the confirmation, the title deed) of the things we hope for, being the proof of things we do not see and the conviction of their reality (faith perceiving as real fact, what is not revealed to the senses). *(Hebrews 11:1)*

When you have the title deed to something, it means that you own it. You have the title deed (promise) of healing and it certainly is not revealed to the senses. That is were your faith comes in.

Since we consider and look not to the things that are seen, but to the things that are unseen; for the things that are visible are temporal (brief and fleeting, but the things that are invisible are deathless and everlasting. *(2 Corinthians 4:18)*

Everything you see around you will someday vanish. It's what you can't see that is real. These precious and exceedingly great promises are more real than what you are seeing and feeling.

You can't see your promise of healing, but it was already done for you on the cross.

For whatever is born of God (you) is victorious over the world; and this is the victory that conquers the world, even our Faith.

(1 John 5:4)

At one particular visit to the doctor, he told me that he believed that the source of my problem was the mercury fillings that were in my teeth. He said I needed to go and have them all removed. Well, needless to say just about every tooth in my mouth had mercury fillings, and they had been there since I was in my teens and early twenties. I was pretty upset when I left his office.

That evening when I went to bed, I opened the scriptures to the book of *2 Chronicles 16:12* that said, "In the thirty-ninth year of his reign, King Asa was diseased in his feet, until his disease became very severe; yet in his disease he did not seek the Lord, but relied on the physicians."

Verse 13 says, "And Asa slept with his fathers, dying in the forty-first year of his reign." Just two years later. That was my first revelation.

Could it be that I was putting my trust and reliance on this doctor instead of God? Yes, I was. In my prayer time with the Lord the next morning, I asked the Lord to forgive me and began my walk of Faith.

I decided that I would not have those fillings removed, and trust God. I called it my first crossroad. I decided to walk by faith and not by sight (circumstances).

For as the human body apart from the Spirit is lifeless, so faith apart from its works of obedience, is also dead.

(James 2:26)

Here is a Revelation. Romans 10:17 says, "Faith (absolute trust, confidence and reliance on God) comes from hearing (first you have to hear what is being told) and hearing by the word (Rhema) spoken from God, Himself." That word Rhema in Greek means to speak, utterance, a matter or topic, saying, command.

That Rhema (spoken word) comes directly from God, Himself. You can get that (Rhema) spoken word from hearing that still small voice, or by reading the scripture and it quickens your spirit. It comes alive, because it came directly from Him. That is exactly what happened when I opened the Bible and read about King Asa. It became Rhema. God was speaking to me through the scripture.

Now if I hadn't been obedient to what I believed God was saying to me through that scripture about King Asa, I could have ended up dieing just like him. I didn't realize that my faith, trust and reliance were not on God, but on the doctor.

Also, I would have gone through an enormous expense. Besides, having the fillings removed would have broken most of my teeth, because they had been in there for so long.

We must spend time with our Savior, and in the word in order to hear His voice. So, if you want to build, develop and strengthen your faith in any situation, you need a Rhema (spoken) word to be able to stand in the worst of storms.

The reason I am teaching you this is because that is exactly what Jesus did. He did nothing apart from what He heard His Father say to Him. That is why He was so successful in His earthly ministry. He did nothing on His own.

So Jesus answered them by saying, "I assure you, most solemnly I tell you, the Son is able to do nothing of Himself (of His own accord); but He is able to do only what He sees the Father doing, for whatever the Father does is what the Son does in the same way." *(John 5:19)*

I love the scripture in *Mark 2:3-11* where the four friends brought a paralytic to Jesus by digging a hole in the roof above Him and lowered him down through the roof of the house where Jesus was.

When Jesus saw the faith of the four friends (their confidence in God through Him), He said to the paralyzed man: "Son, your sins are forgiven you and put away. The penalty is remitted and the sense of guilt removed, and you are made upright and in right standing with God."

The scribes got all bent out of shape, questioning Jesus' authority to forgive sin. Who does he think He is to say this? Only God can remove guilt, remit the penalty, and bestow righteousness.

In verse 9, Jesus said, "Which is easier to say to the paralyzed man, your sins are forgiven and put away, or to say, rise, take up your sleeping pad and start walking about?"

First of all, Jesus wanted them to see who He was and that He had the authority to forgive men's sins. Also, it proves that healing is part of your Salvation. Jesus forgave the man's sins, healing him at the same time, because Salvation is forgiveness of sins, healing and deliverance.

Revelation! Some people, when they get saved, are instantly healed at the same time.

But without Faith it is impossible to please and be satisfactory to Him.

(Hebrews 11:6)

Because of faith, Enoch was caught up and transferred to heaven. He had pleased and been satisfactory to God.

Also, Noah, being forewarned by God concerning events of which as yet there was no visible sign, took heed and diligently and reverently built an ark. It says his faith made him an heir and possessor of righteousness (that relation of being right, into which God puts the person, who has faith).

Sarah, herself, received physical power to conceive a child, even when she was long past the age for it, because she considered (God), who had given her the promise, to be reliable and trustworthy, and true to His word.

What I am teaching and sharing with you could mean the difference between life and death. Jesus told many that he healed; it was their faith that made them whole and be it unto you according to your faith.

I had the awesome opportunity a few years ago to minister at a Women's meeting, when a deaf lady came up for prayer, at the end of the meeting. Her friend said she came expecting that God would open up her ears when I prayed for her. That is exactly what happened. She could hear perfectly. Praise the Lord! She came expecting God to heal her. Expect God to do what He says.

Wait and hope for and expect the Lord; be brave and of good courage and let your heart be stout and enduring. Yes, wait for and hope for and expect the Lord.

There was a woman who had a flow of blood for twelve years. She had endured much suffering under the hands of many physicians, had spent all that she had, and was no better but instead grew worse. Jesus said to her, "Daughter, your faith (your trust and confidence in Me, springing from faith in God) has restored you to health." *(Mark 5:25-34)*

Jesus said to the two blind men, "Do you believe that I am able to do this?" They said "yes". He replied, "According to your faith (trust, reliance on God and His power) be it done unto you." *(Matthew 9:28, 29)*

Jesus asked the blind man in *Luke 18:41* "What do you want Me to do for you?" He said, "Lord, let me receive my sight!" And Jesus said to him, "Receive your sight! Your faith (your trust and confidence that spring from your faith in God) has healed you."

And instantly he received his sight.

Now at Lystra, a man sat who found it impossible to use his feet, for he was crippled from birth and had never walked. He was listening to Paul as he talked, and Paul gazing intently at him and observing that he had faith to be healed, shouted at him, saying, "Stand erect on your feet!" And he leaped up and walked. *(Acts 14:8-10)*

I believe with all my heart that it is not God's will for his people to be sick, diseased, crippled, paralyzed, blind, deaf, mute, feeble minded, etc., because Salvation means healing, deliverance and to (make) whole.

How is God glorified through a sickly, diseased, infirmed, feeble body? I believe He is glorified when that person is healed. For example, *John 9:1* confirms this. There was a man blind from his birth. Jesus' disciples asked him, Rabbi, who sinned, this man or his parents, that he should be born blind?

Jesus answered; "It was not that this man or his parents sinned, but he was born blind in order that the workings of God should be manifested (displayed and illustrated) in him." In other words, so that God would get the glory!

When He had said this, He spat on the ground and made clay (mud) with His saliva, and He spread it as ointment on the man's eyes. And He said to him, "Go wash in the Pool of Siloam" which means Sent. So he went and washed, and came back seeing.

But the just shall live by faith
(Hebrews 10:38)

Some people believe that Paul's thorn in the flesh was a disease or sickness that God sent upon him. The Word tells us that to keep him from being puffed up and too much elated by the exceeding greatness of these revelations, there was given to him a thorn in the flesh, a messenger of satan, to rack and buffet and harass him, to keep him from being excessively exalted.

The word buffet means to rap with the fist. Constantly, the devil was stirring up people and trouble, to have him beaten, whipped and punished. Sickness and disease was not the thorn.

If you read what Paul went through for the Gospel; for example, when he was stoned and they dragged him away thinking he was dead. I wonder what damage was done to his body; possibly his face or eye, could have been disfigured. He was put in prison and beaten to a pulp. He was shipwrecked on an island.

That was great persecution for the Gospel of Jesus Christ. Not all of us are called and appointed to go through that, but there will be persecution for the Gospels sake. Even now children are being persecuted in our schools for having a Bible.

Remember when the young girl at Columbine was shot because she would not renounce Jesus. Persecution for the Gospel is not sickness and disease.

Another question someone asked was what about the baby that King David had with Bathsheba? He took another man's wife and had sex with her. He went as far as to have the husband killed so no one would find out about it. God struck the child that Uriah's wife bore to David, and he was very sick and died. I would think that would be a great lesson for us all. Sin does have consequences. Be sure, your sin will find you out.

Repent of any known sin.

We do not live according to the old Law of sin and death. Remember, those who are in Christ, live according to the Law of the Spirit of Life, healing, divine health, deliverance, safety, rescue, preservation, prosperity, wholeness, liberty and freedom.

For the Law of the Spirit of life which is in Christ Jesus has freed me from the Law of sin and death. (Romans 8:2) The Promises were given to us to escape from the corruption that is in the world. *(2 Peter 1:4)*

CHAPTER 4

FAITH AND PATIENCE INHERITS THE PROMISES OF GOD

*H*ebrews. 6:12 tells us that, in order that you may not grow disinterested and become spiritual sluggards, but imitators, behaving as do those who through faith (by their leaning on the entire personality on God, in Christ, in absolute trust and confidence in His power, wisdom, and goodness), and by practice of patient endurance and waiting, are now inheriting the promises. *(Hebrews 6:12)*

For you have need of steadfast patience and endurance, so that you may perform and fully accomplish the will of God, and thus receive and carry away (and enjoy to the fullest) what is promised. (Hebrews 10:36)

The Promise is Healing and Divine Health

The reason this is so serious is that not everyone gets a supernatural healing instantly in the healing lines. Just because you didn't get the manifestation right away, does not mean that you are not healed.

It merely means that you may have to walk it out through faith like I had to.

Jesus is the author and the perfecter of our faith. He wants to grow and develop our trust, confidence and reliance upon Him. He will perfect our faith, if we will let Him.

Almost two years had gone by and my faith was growing stronger. In my prayer time with the Lord I would hear him speak to me in that (Rhema) still small voice, "The enemy doesn't give up easy."

Satan knows whether <u>you</u> know that you know. He knows whether you have the revelation that you have already been healed by His stripes, by what you say and do.

Impatience will short-circuit your Faith. "Well, I guess I didn't get healed so I'll do it my way." "It's taking too long." If that is the case, you could end up regretting your decision.

Those who wait upon the Lord shall renew their strength. They shall mount up with wings as eagles, they shall run and not be weary, they shall walk and not become faint or tired.

(Isaiah 40:31)

You might have experienced your healing when someone prayed for you, but then a symptom returned, and the enemy convinced you that you didn't get healed. Some people only get as far as the parking lot before the enemy steals it away.

It is similar to the parable of the sower. While anyone is hearing the Word of the kingdom and does not grasp and comprehend it, the evil one (devil) comes and snatches away what was sown in his heart. The Word is seed. *(Luke 8:11, 12)*

All of these words that you are reading and taking into your heart are good seed. I pray right now, in the name of Jesus, that these words will stay in your heart and produce a hundredfold fruit and the manifestation of your healing.

Some people have been prayed for and healed, but then the enemy puts the symptoms back on them and they believe the lie and lose their healing. You have to know how to keep your healing. That is why Redemptive Revelation and knowing the strategies of the enemy are so important.

How do you get a testimony without a test? Our faith will be tested! I asked the Lord one time, "Why do things take so long?" He replied, "So that the genuineness of your faith may be tested." Your faith is infinitely more precious than the perishable gold which is tested and purified by fire. This proving of your faith is intended to redound to your praise and glory and honor when Jesus Christ the Messiah, the anointed One is revealed!" *(1 Peter 1:7)*

As for God, His way is perfect! The word of the Lord is tested and tried.

(Psalm 18:30)

Blessed, happy to be envied, is the man who is patient under trial and stands up under temptation, for when he has stood the test and been approved, he will receive the victor's crown of life which God has promised to those who love Him. *(James 1:12)*

What does it mean to be persistent in your Faith? Persistence means to go on resolutely (firmly, determined in purpose, steadfast or stubbornly, persistent manner) in spite of difficulties: Persevere!

You have a whole cloud of witnesses up there cheering you on and rooting for you. You will reap if you faint not! Even when nothing is happening and it looks dead, hopeless; will you continue to believe God?

Put yourself in Jairus's place. In *Mark 5:22* Jairus, a ruler of the synagogue, came up and prostrated himself at Jesus feet. His little daughter was at the point of death. He asked Jesus to come and lay hands on her so she would live.

To make a long story short, Jesus got sidetracked with the woman with the issue of blood, and while he was still speaking to her, someone from the ruler's house, said to Jairus, "Your daughter has died." "Why bother and distress the Teacher any further?" Wow! What would you do at that point?

What would you do if the doctor gave you the report that you were going to die from a disease that is fatal? That is why it is so important to have Redemptive Revelation of what has already been done for you, and to hear that Rhema spoken word from God. He will speak, if you will listen and obey.

Jesus overheard and ignored what was said and told Jairus, "Do not be seized with alarm or struck with fear; only keep on BELIEVING."

They laughed and jeered at Him when he told them that she was only asleep, so he put everyone out except the mother and father and those that were with him and gripping her hand said, "Arise" and instantly she got up and started walking.

Even when the doctor says there is no cure, or you only have a short time to live, you have already been healed!

Don't let divine delays rob you of your healing, vision and dream. Even when Jesus heard that his friend Lazarus was sick, He still stayed two days longer in the same place where He was. Lazarus had already been in the tomb four days. Perfect!

Now, the son of God may be glorified through and by it. Jesus said, "Take away the stone." Martha, the sister of the dead man, exclaimed! "But Lord, by this time he throws off an offensive odor, for he has been dead four days!"

Jesus said to her, "Did I not tell you and PROMISE you that if you would BELIEVE and rely on Me, you would see the glory of God!" "Lazarus, come out!" Read the rest of the story for yourself. *(John Chapter 11)*

My point is that even when the doctors tell you there is nothing that can be done, or there is no other way besides surgery, it is not true.

Who are you going to believe?

CHAPTER 5

FAITH WITHOUT WORKS IS DEAD

I understand now what it means to fight the good fight of faith. We do not wrestle against flesh and blood, but against powers, principalities, and rulers in high places. *(Ephesians 6:12)*

> *For as the human body apart from the spirit is lifeless, so faith apart from its works of obedience is also dead.*
>
> **(James 2:26)**

I call Faith and Works the Dynamic Duo! Faith and works (actions of obedience) are like Bonnie and Clyde, Laurel and Hardy, Batman and Robin, Snoopy and Charlie. They function together. You need both to get results.

I heard the Lord say to me (Rhema) that "If you really believe it, you will act upon it." In other words, put action to what you believe.

James also wrote, "But be doers of the Word (obey the message), and not merely listeners of it, betraying yourselves into deception by reasoning contrary to the truth." When you hear God, obey. Don't try to reason things out. *(James 1:22)*

About two years had gone by and one day I got a phone call from the doctor telling me that there wasn't anything more that he could do for me, and that I needed to have my thyroid removed or have it killed with radiation and take drugs the rest of my life. That night I went to bed, and when I awoke in the morning the Lord put two scriptures on my heart (Rhema).

The first scripture was *Matthew 14:28-31*. And Peter answered Him, "Lord if it is You, command me to come to You on the water." He said, "Come"! So Peter got out of the boat and walked on the water, and he came toward Jesus.

Verse 30: But when he perceived and felt the strong wind, he was frightened, and as he began to sink he cried out. "Lord, save me from death."

God did not give us a spirit of fear, but He gave us a Spirit of power, love and a sound mind.

(2 Timothy 1:7)

Verse 31: Instantly, Jesus reached out His hand and caught and held him, saying to him, "Oh you of little faith, why did you doubt?" Don't be too hard on Peter. How would he ever become a water-walker, and perform the signs and wonders that he did, if he didn't practice.

You may never practice your faith by walking on actual water, but you will have plenty of opportunity to practice it through the circumstances of life.

We walk by faith and not by sight
(2 Corinthians 5:7)

Is God calling you to get out of the boat of your circumstances and walk on water? Is He calling you to put action to your faith, and to completely trust Him with your life? If so, take authority over that spirit of fear and do exactly what He tells you to do.

Are you willing to be shown (proof) you foolish (unproductive, spiritually deficient) fellow, that faith apart from good works (actions of obedience), is inactive and ineffective and worthless? *(James 2:20)*

Was not our forefather Abraham shown to be justified (made acceptable to God) by his works when he brought to the alter, as an offering, his own son, Isaac? *(James 2:21)*

You see that his faith was cooperating with his works, and his faith was completed and reached its supreme expression when he implemented it by good works, (actions of obedience). *(James 2:22)*

You are justified (pronounced righteous before God) through what you do and not alone through faith. You are justified through your works of obedience, as well as by what you believe. *(James 2:20-22, 24)*

I knew God was speaking to me through these scriptures. My faith would be dead if I didn't exercise it. It was good practice and training by the Holy Spirit of God, just like Peter's training. The Holy Spirit was telling me to get out of the boat and walk on water. "You were already healed by My stripes." "If you really believe it, then act upon it." Remember, the promise is obtained through Faith.

Your actions reveal what you believe.

What if the woman with the issue of blood would have stayed home that day: *wishing and hoping, thinking and praying, planning and dreaming and wishing on a star. It won't get you very far, but if you'll believe God's word you will see. All you've got to do is believe it, speak it, and do it, and you will be free. (Song)*

She heard that Jesus was in town. Remember, faith comes by hearing. She heard the reports of all the wondrous miracles and healings that He was doing. Secondly, she believed it in her heart. Thirdly, she spoke what she believed.

She kept saying to herself, "I know that if I just touch (action) the hem of His garment, I will be healed!"

My husband and I were at a meeting in St. Louis, Missouri recently, where I had a divine encounter with a woman named LaVeeda. We had a wonderful time sharing with one another. She told me all the wonderful things God was doing in her life. We were down in the lobby of the hotel when we separated and I went up to the eighth floor.

A short time later, as I was walking to my room, I heard someone singing a song I was familiar with and I started singing it also. Come to find out it was LaVeeda and we joined in the song together. She began telling me about the disk in her back and the pain she was having. As she was explaining, I sensed the presence of the Lord and told her that God wanted to heal her back.

I laid hands on her back and prayed. Then, I told her to do something she couldn't do before. She bent down and touched the floor. When she stood up, with tears in her eyes, she said that she was not able to do that before. God had healed her right there in the hallway on the eighth floor of the hotel. We jumped and danced together. You see, she put her faith into action when I told her to do something she couldn't do before. Your actions reveal what you believe.

I remember one time ministering in a church, using rose petals as a point of contact. Later a lady told me that, as she took the rose petal, God healed her hip. She didn't need that hip operation after all. Praise the Lord! When she reached out for the rose petal, it was like reaching for the hem of His garment.

On another one of our out-of-town meetings, I used rose petals again, as a point of contact. Several months later, I heard from a woman that was healed of depression and compulsive overeating during that event.

I had to make a decision. Would I believe the word (Rhema) that God gave me, and be obedient to what God was telling me to do, or the devil's fear tactics and symptoms? We must practice our faith. You mean like a piano and a sport? Yes, the word tells us that we may discern daily, by experience, that we are coming to know Him, and becoming better acquainted with Him, if we keep (bear in mind, observe, practice) His teachings, precepts and commandments. *(1 John 2:3)*

Also, that solid food is for full-grown men, for those whose senses and mental faculties are trained by practice to discriminate and distinguish between what is morally good and noble and what is evil and contrary either to divine law (Law of the spirit of Life) or human law (Law of sin and death).

We must exercise and practice to become skilled at distinguishing. Is this from God or from the devil? Faith is like a muscle, if you don't exercise it, it becomes flabby and weak.

We must (practice) train our senses (sight, what we hear) so that we do not fall prey to the enemy. I must get skillful at this because the word says to add your diligence (to the divine promises), employ every effort in exercising your faith.

I took the medication that I was on to regulate the thyroid and cut it down gradually to ¾, ½,

¼, each week, and threw the rest away. A week went by after I stopped taking the drug and the symptoms came back like a flood.

---
*We don't go by circumstances,
what we feel or see.*

CHAPTER 6

FEAR, DOUBT AND UNBELIEF

When you get ready to put your faith into action, you will always be met with resistance. The enemy does not want you to get the victory. He will throw everything at you that He can.

God did not give us a spirit of fear, but a spirit of power, love and a sound mind. *(2 Timothy 1:7)*. God calls it a spirit.

Fear is false evidence appearing real.

Joseph's father, Jacob, believed his sons when they came back with False Evidence Appearing Real. They brought back Joseph's coat with animal blood on it. Very powerful evidence wouldn't you agree? Jacob didn't have a very happy life for a long time. *(Genesis 37:5-8, 31-35)*

Satan is a counterfeit, master manipulator and deceiver. That evil spirit will try to control and manipulate you to do it his way instead of God's way.

He'll tell you it's never going to work. God isn't going to do what He said He would. You will always be that way and things will never change.

When fear is in operation, Satan is at work. Fear opens the door for the devil to get involved in your life, causing sickness, disease, death, confusion, phobias (an irrational persistent fear or dread, etc). You have given him (Satan) permission, through fear, to get into your life. You have opened a door to Him that must be shut!

Fear can change the outcome of your situation. It can make you do things you wouldn't normally do.

Fear is his number one weapon. He will tell you that you are going to die if you stop taking your medication, or this or that will happen. Fear doesn't come from God. It is the opposite of Faith. It can be gripping and tormenting. But, who is the tormenter? The spirit of fear can rearrange the situation and bring the wrong result. Fear causes us to try to do it a different way than God's way.

Here are a few examples:

Fear of:

1. Man
2. Failure
3. Success
4. Losing a job
5. Death
6. Animals
7. Washing hands (Phobia)
8. Heights
9. The Unknown
10. Closed-in space
11. Sickness & disease
12. God won't do what He said

I knew a lady some years ago who always wore gloves on her hands. She had a phobia (fear) of germs to the point of wearing cloth gloves wherever she went.

There is no fear in love (dread does not exist) but full-grown (complete, perfect) love turns fear out of doors and expels every trace of terror. *(1st John 4:18)*

I grew up with an extreme lack of self-confidence and fear of people. I couldn't talk in front of people. I was afraid of my own shadow, so-to-speak. God has delivered me and set me free and I know the more I practice unconditional love for people the more free I will become.

Remember, we said the suggestion (thought) of oppression is presented, and then becoming frightened by the spirit of fear, the disease or sickness secures a foothold (stronghold). The devil wants you to think his way. There is a symptom or pain, you receive it, start speaking it and then act upon it.

> *For the thing which I greatly fear comes upon me, and that of which I am afraid befalls me.*
> **(Job 3:25)**

As soon as I had made the decision to walk by faith and throw the drug away, the devil was right there to tell me that this would happen and that would happen and that I would die. I could feel the spirit of fear trying to take hold of me, and to keep me from my promise of healing.

The other scripture that God revealed (Rhema) to me was about the children of Israel going into the Promised Land. The scouts came back with an evil report and the children of Israel became full of fear, doubt and unbelief. (*Numbers 13 and 14*)

God had given them a promise and that promise was the land of milk and honey, good land. The promise was theirs, but they had to go in and possess it. The word *possess* means to take it by force. They had to do something. God said that He would drive out the inhabitants before them, but they still had to go in and fight. The only two who believed God were Joshua and Caleb.

You also have to possess (take it by force) your promise. You have to put action to what you believe.

We do not wrestle against flesh and blood but against powers, principalities and rulers in high places.

Well, to make a long story short, that whole generation died off in the wilderness because they did not believe God.

Fear, doubt and unbelief kept them out.

It takes revelation to see the similarity of the children of Israel and the people of God today. Fear, doubt and unbelief caused the Israelites to miss the promise (land) and perish, die in the wilderness.

Fear, doubt and unbelief cause the people of God to miss the promise of (healing) and perish in the wilderness.

The Israelites saw the giants in the land, which caused them to be fearful, full of doubt and unbelief. They saw themselves as grasshoppers in their own sight. We hear, see or feel the symptoms, report of the doctor; and become fearful, instead of believing God. They went by what they saw and we do the same thing.

In *Genesis 3:1*, "And he (Satan) said to the woman, "Can it really be that God has said, you shall not eat from every tree of the garden?" Do you see how he is trying to make Eve doubt what God said? Can it really be that is what He said?

I remember one time, years ago; I was in a figure skating competition and did terribly. I doubted myself through the whole program. I was so upset. Afterward, I went to the Lord and asked Him about it. He said there was a spirit of self-doubt operating against me.

I had entered into His rest, knowing that I was already healed and that I would stand no matter what. Whose report will you believe? The devil, the doctors, man, symptoms, circumstances, or God?

In *Matthew 13*, Jesus could not do many works of power in His own home town because of their unbelief (their lack of faith in the divine mission of Jesus).

Unbelief will keep you from your healing

No unbelief or distrust made him (Abraham) waver or doubtingly question concerning the promise of God, but he grew strong and was empowered by faith as he gave praise and glory to God. *(Romans 4:20)*

Fully satisfied and assured that God was able and mighty to keep His word and to do what He had promised. *(Romans 4:21)*

Therefore, while the promise of entering His rest still holds and is offered today, let us be afraid to distrust it, lest any of you should think he has come too late and has come short of reaching it. *(Hebrews 4:1)*

For indeed we have had the glad tidings, the Gospel of God, proclaimed to us just as truly as they, the Israelites of old did when the good news of deliverance from bondage came to them. The message they heard did not benefit them, because it was not mixed with faith, the leaning on the entire personality on God in absolute trust and confidence in His power, wisdom and goodness, by those who heard it. Neither were they united in faith with the ones, Joshua and Caleb, who heard and did believe. *(Hebrews 4:2)*

For we who have believed (past tense) that your healing was already done, do rest in accordance with His declaration that those who did not believe should not enter when He said, "As I swore in My wrath, they shall not enter My rest." And this He said although His works had been completed and prepared and waiting for all who would believe from the foundation of the world. *(Hebrews 4:3)*

His works have already been completed and prepared and waiting for all who would believe from the foundation of the world.

The word (works) means an act. We said earlier that Redemption in the Greek means, the act, ransom in full, i.e., riddance or salvation, deliverance, redemption through His blood.

His works (healing, divine health, deliverance, safety, rescue, preservation, wholeness, all the promises of God, etc.) have already been done at the cross. It has been accomplished and waiting for all those who believe God. Because they do believe, they can rest, knowing that it has been completed.

Sometimes it takes much (labor) to believe God. We must labor to get into that rest to believe God. Once I have entered into that rest, it's just a matter of time before I see the manifestation of that promise.

My husband and I spent a couple of days in New Hampshire recently enjoying some rest before our next ministry in New York. I was praying and meditating, sensing the presence of the Lord. I looked out toward the mountain and the top of it was covered with a cloud. I couldn't see it.

Then the cloud moved upward and I could clearly see the top of the mountain.

I heard the Lord say that your promise is there, just like the top of the mountain, but you can't see it.

We walk by faith, not by sight

For he who has once entered God's rest also has ceased from the weariness and pain of human labors, just as God rested from those labors, peculiarly His own. *(Hebrews 4:10)*

Let us, therefore, be zealous and exert ourselves and strive diligently to enter that rest (to believe God) to know and experience it for ourselves that no one may fall or perish by the same kind of unbelief and disobedience (into which those in the wilderness fell). *(Hebrews 4:11)*

> ***And He (Jesus) did not do many works of power there, because of their unbelief (their lack of faith in the divine mission of Jesus).***
> **Matthew 13:58**

Weeks had gone by, even months, since I stopped the drug to control my thyroid.

It didn't matter, because I had entered into His rest knowing I was healed. I heard God say, (Rhema) "Don't go by what you feel, or see happening."

CHAPTER 7

HOLD FAST TO YOUR CONFESSION OF FAITH
(Hebrews 4:14)

I believe, therefore, I speak! *(Psalm 116:10)*

For the Word that God speaks is alive and full of power, making it active; operative, energizing, and effective; it is sharper than any two-edged sword, penetrating to the dividing line of the "breath of life (soul) and the immortal spirit, and of joints and marrow (of the deepest parts of our nature) exposing and sifting and analyzing and judging the very thoughts and purposes of the heart. *(Hebrews 4:12)*

And God said, let there be light; and there was light.

(Genesis 1:1-3)

This tells me that the Word of God, that I speak, penetrates into my joints and marrow and into the deepest parts of me. Our words will bring us life and healing or bring death and curses. This chapter on words is most vital to walking out your healing.

The word tells us in *Proverbs 18:20, 21*, that a man's (moral) self shall be filled with the fruit of his mouth; and the consequences of his words he must be satisfied (whether good or evil).

In *Verse 21* it says that "Death and life are in the power of the tongue, and they who indulge in it shall eat the fruit of it for death or life." You will either speak death to yourself or someone else, or life to yourself or someone else.

Many years ago, the Lord taught me about receiving words, negative things that people would say to me.

As I was pulling out of my driveway one day to go to the ice skating rink for practice before a competition, my neighbor, who lived across the street, yelled to me "break a leg."

You may think that it's just a saying, but I am here to tell you how powerful your words are! That day during my practice time at the ice rink, I fell and broke my ankle. I would not be going to the competition. Now, I verbally say, so that my ears can hear "I loose, melt and dissolve those words and I don't receive them."

In *Matthew 16:22, 23,* Jesus turned away from Peter and said to him, "Get behind Me Satan! You are in My way (an offense and a hindrance and a snare to Me); for you are minding what partakes not of the nature and quality of God, but of men."

Jesus was speaking directly to Peter. Some people will say things to you that can become a hindrance and a snare to your life. You must rebuke those words.

My son, attend to my words; consent and submit to my sayings. Let them not depart from your sight; keep them in the center of your heart.

For they are life to those who find them, healing and health to all their flesh. *(Proverbs 4:20-22)*

Start watching what you say. Pay close attention to the words that come out of your mouth. Do they line up with God's word, or do they line up with what you feel, see, hear, or the circumstances.

Do you speak what the world says, or do you speak what God says? For by your words you will be justified and acquitted, and by your words you will be condemned and sentenced.

(Matthew 12:37)

God says, "By His wounds you were healed and that He bore your sickness and disease in His body on the cross." Is that what you are saying, or are you confessing the problem and telling everyone about the sickness and disease you have? As soon as a symptom or diagnosis comes, you will either claim it as yours, or speak what the word of God speaks.

You are snared with the words of your lips; you are caught by the speech of your mouth. (Proverbs 6:2)

There are those who speak rashly, like the piercing of a sword, but the tongue of the wise brings healing. (Proverbs 12:18)

So many of God's children are confessing everything the world says such as: "I better get my flu shot this year. I don't want to get the flu." They confess every negative thing on themselves and wonder why. They have taken that sickness, disease and claimed it for their own, by the words of their mouth.

I remember one time, my husband and I were visiting some family members. We stayed overnight and I kept the window open all night while it was damp outside. I mentioned it in the morning and the woman of the house said, with all forcefulness, "You will catch your death and get sick." Well, I didn't rebuke those words and send them back and on the way home my throat started getting sore and I couldn't breathe out of my nose.

I kept singing over and over again, "In the name of Jesus, in the name of Jesus, we have the victory, in the name of Jesus, demons will have to flee. Do you know what God can do? Do you know that He died for you? In the mighty name of Jesus, we have the victory."

By the time we arrived home, about 12 hours later, I was completely well. The symptoms were gone and we stopped at a Sonic for a *Blast*. What a battle that was!

This is my comfort and consolation in my affliction; that your word has revived me and given me life.
(Psalm 119:50)

You cannot receive the curses and the negative things that people say so that the devil can't get a stronghold against you, and you will not have to go through the battle. It would have been much easier to not have received it in the first place. Reject those negative words.

A gentle tongue (with its healing power) is a tree of life, but willful contrariness in it breaks down the spirit. I didn't know my tongue was likened to a tree. Let's take that a step further. *(Proverbs 15:4)*

Jesus said that He is the Vine and we are the branches. Apart from Him, we can do nothing. He prunes all the branches that do not bear fruit. Trees bear fruit, but what kind of fruit are they producing. You shall know a tree, by its fruit.

Peace, peace, to him who is far off (both Jew and Gentile) and to him who is near! Says the Lord; I create the fruit of his lips, and I will heal him (make his lips blossom anew with speech in thankful praise). *(Isaiah 57:19)*

I want my words to produce good fruit, good results and not bad results.

Your tongue is like a tree according to *Matthew 12:33*. "Either make the tree (tongue) sound (healthy and good) and its fruit sound (healthy and good) or make the tree (tongue) rotten (diseased and bad); for the tree is known and recognized and judged by its fruit."

Also, our heart and tongue are connected, because God's word says that out of the heart, the mouth speaks. *(Matthew 12:34)* What you believe, will come out of your mouth whether for good or bad.

Yes, my heart will rejoice when your lips speak right things. *(Proverbs 23:16)*

My son, attend to my words; consent and submit to my sayings. Let them not depart from your sight; keep them in the center of your heart. For they are life to those who find them, healing and health to all their flesh
(Proverbs 4:20-23)

For example, the Bible tells us about the tongue being like the rudder of a ship. The rudder steers the ship wherever the captain wants it to go. He will steer it into deep water, or into shallow water and hit a rock.

Think of yourself as the captain of your ship (body).

Your tongue (rudder) will take you into sickness and disease, calamity, decay, malady, infirmity and every other evil thing, unless you practice steering the rudder by God's word. *(James 3:4-6)*

That goes for everything. Do you think it's easy? Try it! It takes much practice, work and diligence. The word says that adding your diligence to the divine promises employ every effort in exercising your faith. *(2 Peter 1:5).*

God says in His word, "As it is written, I have made you (Abraham) the father of many nations." He was appointed our father in the sight of God in whom he believed, who gives life to the dead and speaks of the non-existent things that He has foretold and promised as if they already existed. *(Romans 4:17, 19-21)*

That scripture is telling us that God speaks of the things that are non-existent (Promise of healing). It hasn't manifested yet. A good example of speaking what God speaks even when yet there is no evidence.

Declaring the end and the result from the beginning saying, "My counsel shall stand, and I will do all My pleasure and purpose." *(Isaiah 46:10)*

You can declare the answer, which you haven't seen yet, or you can declare the problem. Your healing has already been done for you and with your tongue, God will cause it to manifest. Do you believe it? Then decree it and declare it. We reap what we sew. Words are seeds; they will produce good or bad fruit. There is nothing worse than a rotten apple.

A man's moral self shall be filled with the fruit of his mouth; and with the consequence of his words he must be satisfied (whether good or evil).

(Proverbs 18:20-21)

He who brings an offering of praise and thanksgiving, honors and glorifies Me; and he who orders his way (conversation) aright, to him I will demonstrate the Salvation of God. *(Psalm 50:23)*. The word (way) in the Hebrew is Derek which means course of life, action, conduct, conversation.

What is the Salvation of God? Healing, Divine Health, Deliverance, Wholeness, Rescue, Safety, Preservation, and Protection, etc. All the Promises of God. Awesome!

Order your conversation aright and God will demonstrate His healing power. Are words important? You better believe it! Jesus calmed the storm with His words. You can calm the storm with yours.

Pleasant words are as a honeycomb, sweet to the mind and healing to the body.

(Proverbs 16:24)

Whosoever shall say unto this mountain. Well, what is that mountain in your life? Is it sickness and disease, a malady or infirmity, sorrow, rejection, addiction? Then say unto that mountain be thou removed and cast into the sea and shall not doubt in his heart, but shall BELIEVE those things which he SAYS, they shall come to pass. *(Mark 11:23)*

If you BELIEVE in your heart and confess with your mouth, that God raised Jesus from the dead, you will be saved, (healed, delivered, set free, rescued, preserved, kept safe, made whole).

If you BELIEVE in your heart and confess with your mouth, *1 Peter 2:24, Matthew 8:17, Psalm 103:3, Isaiah 53:5*, you will see the result.

Make it personal and say Lord, you forgive all of my sin and heal all my diseases. You carried away my sickness and disease and by your stripes I am and have been healed.

Lord, your word says that it was already done for me at the cross. If you believe it, then start speaking it.

Speak to that pain or symptom to be gone in the name of Jesus. Better yet, do not receive it in the first place. Reject it and command it to go in the name of Jesus. The devil knows if you believe it or not. Remember, the word that you speak (God's word) penetrates all the way to the joints and marrow. Speak to the symptom and command it to go.

I remember, a long while back, the joint in my knee would give out unexpectantly, when I was walking along. It was quite painful. I would just rebuke it and not receive it; speaking God's word that by His stripes I was healed. This went on for several years until, I don't remember when, it just wasn't there anymore.

At one of my dance practices there was a woman who was having pain in her knees and it was very uncomfortable for her to practice. The Holy Spirit led me to stop the practice and have her lay hands on her own knees and repeat the words that I spoke: *"Devil, I reject these symptoms. I don't receive them. You are a liar and I command the pain to go in the name of Jesus."*

I instructed her to start dancing, and instantly the pain was gone and she started dancing around and telling everyone it was gone. She learned how to take the authority herself.

Remember: I believe, therefore I speak!

CHAPTER 8

HINDRANCES TO YOUR PROMISE

*I*f you're not seeing the results to your promise of healing, it may be that there is unforgiveness in your heart, without you realizing it. Our hearts are deceitful above all else. *(Jeremiah 17:9)*

I was sitting at a table one day waiting for the public session at the ice rink to start. I started a conversation with a woman, who was there with her grandson. I noticed that she had a walker and it was extremely hard for her to get around. She was so proud of her family and was telling me all about them.

I tried to just listen without interjecting. She told me about the terrible pain she was having due to arthritis. It had disabled her from freely moving around. I shared my testimony of my healing of graves disease.

While I was sharing, I began to think about the root cause of the arthritis; "A broken spirit dries up the bones." *(Proverbs 17:22)* I began to share with her that sometimes unforgiveness causes arthritis in a person. Well, all of a sudden, she began to cry.

Tears were running from her eyes, and she said, "They hurt me so bad." She said that her family had hurt her, but we didn't get into exactly what they did, and I told her that if she would forgive them, that God would heal her.

I instructed her to bring each name before God and to choose to forgive each one, and to ask God to please help her to let them go, release them to God. This would be an act of obedience on her part, which sometimes is not always easy. God tells us that if we do not forgive one another, He will not forgive us, and I believe that holds back the promises.

There is only one thing impossible for God. He cannot tell a lie.

God is not a man, that He should tell or act a lie, neither the son of man, that He should feel repentance or compunction for what He has promised. Has He said and shall He not do it? Or has He spoken and shall He not make it good? *(Numbers 23:19)*

Now, I was in the ninth month of standing. I knew that I was healed, and I began to see some of the symptoms go away.

For instance, the tremors in my body subsided and I began to see my strength returning. My weight began to increase. There was still one symptom that continued, and that was the throbbing in my ears. This is not the time to give up and settle for less.

I love *1 Kings 18* regarding Ahab and Elijah. It did not rain for a long time. The famine was severe in Samaria. In verse *21*, Elijah came near to all the people and said, "How long will you halt and limp between two opinions?" "If the Lord is God, follow Him! But if Baal, then follow him."

***How long will you halt and limp
between two opinions?***

Will you believe the opinion of the doctor, circumstances, symptoms, what you see, feel or hear, or the Promise of God?

Sometimes people will not believe even when they see someone raised from the dead. In *Luke 16:19*, there was a certain rich man who habitually clothed himself in purple and fine linen and reveled and feasted and made merry in splendor every day.

At the gate of his house, dropped down and left there, was a destitute man named Lazarus, reduced to begging for alms and covered with ulcerated sores. The dogs even came and licked his sores.

They both died and the rich man ended up in Hades and saw Lazarus in the arms of Abraham being comforted. There was a great chasm between them so no one could pass over. The rich man asked Abraham to send Lazarus to his brothers so that they would not end up in that place of torment, and Abraham said, "They have Moses and the Prophets; let them hear and listen to them."

In Verse 31, He said, "If they do not hear and listen to Moses and the Prophets, neither will they be persuaded and convinced and BELIEVE (even) if someone should rise from the dead." Can you imagine, even if someone came back from the dead, some people would not believe.

"What are we to do, that we may habitually be working the works of God?" "What are we to do to carry out what God requires?" *(John 6:28)*

Verse 29 – Jesus replied, "This is the work (service) that God asks of you; that you BELIEVE in the one whom He has sent."

"That you cleave to, trust, rely on, and have faith in His messenger."

Verse 30 – Therefore, they said to Him, "What sign (miracle, wonderwork) will you perform then, so that we may see it and BELIEVE and rely on and adhere to you?" "What supernatural work have You to show what You can do?"

Verse 31 – "But as I told you, although you have seen Me, still you do not believe, trust and have faith." All they wanted was some kind of sign instead of just believing in Him.

Are you looking for a sign?

In the ninth month, God told me to hold a Healing Encounter at the Ice Sports Complex in Ellenton, Florida. God used me to bring healing and deliverance to others.

That last symptom lasted right up until the night of the meeting. Do not settle for partial healing. Stand, in faith, until every last symptom is gone.

I was completely and totally healed without surgery, radiation or having to take drugs the rest of my life. Praise His Holy Name for the victory!

Have you ever heard the statement: A person with an experience is never at the mercy of a person with an argument? I don't have to argue with anyone. I am living proof that God's Promise of healing is true to all who will believe and take Him at His word.

BELIEVE

I also want to add that some people have had an infirmity for so long that they have learned to live with it. It becomes part of who they are. For instance; the man at the pool of Bethesda. In the alcoves, colonnades and doorways lay a great number of sick folks, and at appointed seasons an angel would go down into the pool and move and stir up the water. Whoever stepped in first after the stirring of the water was healed.

There was a certain man there who had suffered with a deep-seated and lingering disorder for thirty-eight years. When Jesus noticed him lying there, knowing that he had already been a long time in that condition, He said to him, "Are you really in earnest about getting well?" Why would Jesus say that?

I believe that the man had given up. He had learned to live with it. He had excuses why he couldn't get into the water.

If the angel came at appointed seasons, you would think, after thirty-eight years, he would have known and made his way to the water ahead of time. Jesus said to him, "Get up!" "Pick up your bed and walk!" And He did! *(John 2-9)*

I really don't like to mention this, but it is true. There are those, for one reason or another, who do not want to be healed. For example, they could lose their tax-payer funded government money. If they get healed, then they would no longer be eligible.

I talked with a deaf lady and that is what she told me. That sounds funny doesn't it? If she was deaf, then how could she talk to me? She read lips and wrote it down on paper.

The same is true of a man and woman living together. They do not want to get married because they will lose tax-payer funded government money.

In *2 Kings 5*, it tells about the story of Naaman, commander of the army of the king of Syria. He was a great man with his master, because by him the Lord had given victory to Syria. He was also a mighty man of valor, but he was a leper.

A little maid from Israel waited on Naaman's wife and she said to her mistress, "would that my Lord were with the prophet who is in Samaria, for He would heal him of his leprosy." Naaman went in and told his king, what his wife told him, and the king of Syria said, "Go now, and I will send a letter to the king of Israel."

Verse 8 says that when Elisha, the man of God, heard that the king of Israel had rent his clothes, he sent to the king, asking, why have you rent your clothes? Let Naaman come now to me and he shall know that there is a prophet in Israel. So Naaman came with his horses and chariots and stopped at Elisha's door.

Elisha sent a messenger to him, saying, "Go and wash in the Jordan seven times, and your flesh shall be restored and you shall be clean."

But Naaman was angry and went away and said, "Behold, I thought he would surely come out to me and stand and call on the name of the Lord his God, and wave his hand over the place and heal the leper."

> *When swelling and pride come, then emptiness and shame come also, but with the humble (those who are lowly, who have been pruned or chiseled by trial, and renounce self) are skillful and godly wisdom and soundness.*
>
> **(Proverbs 11:2)**

"Are not Abana and Pharpar, the rivers of Damascus, better than all the waters of Israel? May I not wash in them and be clean?" So he turned and went away in a rage.

Verse 13 says, and his servants came near and said to him, "My father, if the prophet had bid you to do some great thing, would you not have done it?" "How much rather, then, when he says to you, wash and be clean?" Then he went down and dipped himself seven times in the Jordan, as the man of God had said, and his flesh was restored like that of a little child, and he was clean.

Then Naaman returned to the man of God, he and all his company, and stood before him. He said, "Behold now I know that there is no God in all the earth but in Israel." He almost missed his healing because he thought God should do it a certain way.

So many times we miss God because we put Him in a box and think He should do it a certain way. We try to tell God how to do it. Naaman had a preconceived idea and got angry because it wasn't done the way he thought it should be done.

Also, I detect there was some pride there. Well, the nerve of that man. He couldn't come out and talk to me personally! He's making me go wash in a dirty river! Humble yourself in the sight of the Lord and He will lift you up. God opposes the proud but gives grace to the humble.

Humble yourself in the sight of the Lord and He will lift you up.
(James 4:10)

We have these preconceived ideas of how God should do things, or we try to do it our own way.

We can be in a service or prayer meeting and want to be prayed over for healing, but we think to ourselves: "I can't let that person pray for me." She is a woman, or that's just not the vessel God would send.

My husband and I were staying at a timeshare in Branson, Missouri. We agreed to meet with a staff person for an hour of information and updates in exchange for free tickets.

The gentleman, who was a Christian, mentioned that he was battling with sugar diabetes. I sensed the presence of God and asked him if I could pray for him.

I believed that God wanted to heal him right then and there. He would not let me pray for him and afterward the Lord showed me it was because I was a woman.

David wanted to bring the Ark of God from the house of Abinadab to the City of David. Uzzah and Ahio, sons of Abinadab, drove the new cart. David and all the house of Israel played before the Lord with all their might, with songs, lyres, harps, tambourines, castanets, and cymbals, and when the oxen stumbled and shook it, Uzzah put out his hand to the ark of God and took hold of it.

The anger of the Lord was kindled against Uzzah; and God smote him there for touching the ark, and he died there by the ark of God." *(2 Samuel 6:1-7)*

Obedience is better than sacrifice.
(1 Samuel 15:22)

It can be fatal to try to do it our way, or think that we are helping God. He doesn't need our help. He just wants us to trust, rely and have confidence in Him. Just believe His word and listen to what He says and do it.

The Word tells us to examine ourselves before we partake of communion. In *1 Corinthians 11:28-31*, it tells us that careless and unworthy participation is the reason many of you are weak and sickly, and quite enough of you have fallen into the sleep of death. Make sure there is no unconfessed sin when you participate in the Lord's supper.

Sin can open the door for the devil to afflict you with sickness and disease. For example, the man that Jesus healed in *John 5:14*. Afterward, when Jesus found him in the temple, He said to him, "See, you are well! Stop sinning or something worse may happen to you."

I acknowledged my sin to You, and my iniquity I did not hide. I said, I will confess my transgressions to the Lord. Then You instantly forgave me the guilt and iniquity of my sin.

(Psalm 32:5)

CHAPTER NINE

DO YOU KNOW WHO YOU ARE IN CHRIST?

Many of God's children do not have the revelation of who they are in Christ.

In this chapter, I pray that the Spirit of the Living God, will open to you the revelation that you never have to be sick and diseased another day in your life. That you can walk in divine health just the way Jesus walked in divine health. It takes practice and hard work.

Begin with minor things, such as colds and headaches. Tackle the small things first. Know your authority in Christ. Know where sickness and disease comes from. Never allow the devil to put anything on you again. The moment the devil puts the suggestion there, rebuke him, and do not receive it.

I remember when I first began ministering healing to people, I would ask the Lord to heal that person, because it is God who does the healing, but the Spirit said to me: "You take the authority over those things, in My Name." I have given you the authority over the enemy.

He that is in you is greater than he that is in the world.

(1 John 4:4)

You are a chosen race, a royal priesthood, a dedicated nation, God's own purchased, special people, that you may set forth the wonderful deeds and display the virtues and perfections of Him who called you out of darkness into His marvelous light. *(1 Peter 2:9)*

Remember the scripture that says we have become sharers and partakers of the divine nature when we accepted Jesus. *(2 Peter 1:4)* The Holy Spirit of God now dwells in us. Think of that. We have His supreme nature dwelling in us.

"And if the Spirit of Him, who raised Jesus from the dead dwells in you, then He who raised Christ Jesus from the dead will also restore to life your mortal short-lived, perishable bodies through His Spirit, who dwells in you." *(Romans 8:11)*

The word tells us that "as He is, so am I." "I have been crucified with Christ" (in Him I have shared His crucifixion).

It is no longer I who live, but Christ lives in me; and the life I now live in the body, I live by faith in the Son of God, who loved me and gave Himself up for me. *(Galatians 2:20)*

The same works that Jesus did, we have been commanded to do also. Only greater, because there are more of us. We are to be imitators of Christ.

As He is, so are we in this world.
(1 John 4:17)

For those whom He foreknew (that's you), He also destined from the beginning to be molded into the image of His Son and share inwardly His likeness, that He might become the firstborn among many brethren. *(Romans 8:29)*

I am trying to make you see who you are. We are to live, speak, behave and follow after Jesus' example. You didn't see Him walking around with sickness and disease, malady, infirmity or lack. He carried, took away, and bore your shame, rejection, loneliness, guilt, sorrow and pain and became poor so that you could be rich. He took and carried away your diseases and sickness so you could walk in divine health.

I have told you these things, so that in Me, you may have perfect peace and confidence. In the world, you have tribulation and trials and distress and frustration; but be of good cheer (take courage, be confident, certain, undaunted) for I have overcome the world." *(John 16:33)*

"I have deprived it of power to harm you and have conquered it for you."

(John 16:33)

Jesus conquered, sin, death, sickness, disease, hell and the grave. He has conquered everything for you. Nothing by any means shall harm you. Do you Believe that?

Look at Paul when he was shipwrecked on the Island of Malta. The natives kindled a fire and welcomed and received them all, since it had begun to rain and was cold. Paul had gathered a bundle of sticks, and he was laying them on the fire, when a viper crawled out because of the heat and fastened itself on his hand. Ouch!

When the natives saw the little animal hanging from his hand, they said to one another, doubtless this man is a murderer, for though he has been saved from the sea, justice has not permitted that he should live. Then Paul shook off the small creature into the fire and suffered no evil effects. *(Acts 28:1-6)* What would you do?

Peter was a mere man, who was filled with the Holy Spirit of God, and he walked on water just like Jesus; but he let the circumstances of what he saw and felt, (fear, doubt), caused him to take a swim.

Jesus is our example to follow. The reason the Son of God was made manifest (visible) was to undo (destroy, loosen, and dissolve) the works the devil has done. *(1 John 3:8)*

Jesus gave us the keys of the kingdom of heaven to use on this earth. We also can destroy, loosen, and dissolve the works of the devil and bind up the broken hearted.

The Word tells us in *Mark 16* that these attesting signs will accompany those who believe. The key here is THOSE WHO BELIEVE! In my name they will drive out demons; they will speak in new languages; they will pick up serpents, and even if they drink, eat or touch anything deadly, it will not hurt them; they will lay their hands on the sick, and they will get well. *(Mark 16:17-18)*

They went out and preached the Gospel and the Lord confirmed the message by the attesting signs and miracles. *(Verse 20)*

Jesus only did the things that He heard His Father tell Him. He didn't come to do His own thing. So are we to hear what the Spirit is saying to us.

He will teach, guide, counsel, comfort and give us revelation, insight and understanding in every situation.

Hear what the Spirit is saying.

His Word tells us to trust in the Lord with all of our hearts and to lean not on our own understanding, but to acknowledge Him in ALL of our ways and He will direct our path. *(Proverbs 3:5)* Let's make Jesus the example to follow and imitate.

I want to leave this chapter with one last thought. Think and meditate on this.

He said to them, "You will doubtless, quote to Me this proverb: "Physician heal Yourself?" They called him Physician because he healed people. They wanted to see some of these miracles that they only heard about. *(Luke 4:23)*

If the Great Physician lives within you, you can also speak to that sickness, disease, infirmity, pain, discomfort, rash, infection, and command it to dry up at the root and wither away. Tell that body part to function in the perfection in which God created it to function. Command it to be healed and be whole. As He is, so are you.

Imitate Him and heal yourself with the authority of His word. He was never sick and infirmed and neither should we be.

We were having dance practice at my house one evening and one of the ladies said that her back hurt. I was led to tell her to lay hands on her own back and to speak: "devil I reject and rebuke these symptoms. I don't receive them. I command you and this pain to go in the name of Jesus." Then I instructed her to do a cartwheel. She did and the pain was gone.

Remember, the Word of God is sharper than any two-edged sword, penetrating through to the joints and marrow. It is alive and full of power. Believe it and speak it.

The same Spirit that raised Jesus from the dead lives inside of you.

(Romans 8:11)

CHAPTER 10

WHAT DO YOU THINK?

*T*he battle is won or lost in the mind!

Think on those things that are pure, lovely and of a good report! Are you thinking on the good report of the Lord or the bad report of the devil? What do you think? Your thinking affects your actions. If I think right, I will act right.

As a man thinks in his heart, so is he. That tells me that you are what you think. *(Proverbs 23:7)*

I want to think the Word of God so all that comes out of my mouth is the Word of God. Not what my mother thinks, or what the world says. What does God say about the subject? Have you ever heard the statement, you are what you eat. Well, you are what you think. What are you thinking about?

If you think you are too old, then you will behave that way. If you think you can't do it, you won't. If you think like the world thinks, you'll get what the world gets. If you think (believe) that God doesn't heal all His children, you could die.

The world says: there is no cure for that.

God says: He, Himself, took our weaknesses and infirmities and bore away our diseases. *(Matthew 8:17, Isaiah 53:4-5, 1 Peter 2:24 and Psalm 103:3)*

The world says; you are too old to have a baby.

God says: Look at Abraham and Sarah. *(Romans 4:19-21)*

The world says: you are too old to accomplish that at your age.

God says: I have strength for all things in Christ who empowers me; I am ready for anything and equal to anything through Him who infuses inner strength into me;

I am self-sufficient in Christ's sufficiency. *(Philippians 4:13)*

The world says: you'll never overcome that.

God says: Yet amid all these things, we are more than conquerors and gain a surpassing victory through Him who loved us. *(Romans 8:37)*

The world says: don't put your house up for sale because the market isn't good. You won't get out of it what you put into it.

God says: But Jesus looked at them and said, With men this is impossible, but all things are possible with God. *(Matthew 19:26)*

The world says: I don't have the money for that.

God says: And my God will liberally supply (fill to the full) your every need according to His riches and glory in Christ Jesus. *(Philippians 4:19)*

The world says: the flu is going around. You better get that flu shot.

God says: And thus He fulfilled what was spoken by the prophet Isaiah. He, Himself, took (in order to carry away) our weaknesses and infirmities and bore away our diseases. *(Matthew 8:17)*

The world says: my father died of that, so I probably will.

God says: For as a man thinks in his heart, so is he. *(Proverbs 23:7)* What do you believe (think)? I believe, therefore, I speak. You will speak what you believe.

To think is to have a thought; formulate in the mind, to ponder, to reason, to believe, to suppose, to remember; call to mind, to visualize, imagine, to devise or invent, to consider.

And the Lord said, Behold, they are one people and they have all one language; and this is only the beginning of what they will do, and now nothing they have imagined (think) they can do will be impossible for them. To imagine is to form a mental picture of something not present; think and guess.

Have you ever tried to reason things out?

Because when they knew and recognized Him as God, they did not honor and glorify Him as God, or give thanks, but instead they became futile and godless in their thinking, with vain imaginings, foolish reasoning, and stupid speculations, and their senseless minds were darkened. *(Romans 1:21)*

For example: you have been exposed to someone with the flu, or some infectious disease. The thought comes, now you're going to get it. First of all, where did that thought come from?

Certainly not from God. It doesn't line up with God's Word and certainly not who you are in Christ.

You have one of two choices. You can believe what God says, or what the enemy says. Whatever you believe, you will speak. Strongholds are made up of thoughts. Remember, we said that the devil will make the thought (suggestion). It is up to us what we will do with it.

Or, you can reject it right away, and line up with the Word in 2 *Corinthians 10:5* that says: "In as much as we refute arguments and theories and reasonings and every proud and lofty thing that sets itself up against the true knowledge of God; and we lead every THOUGHT and purpose away captive into the obedience of Christ.

I cast down every thought and imagination and every high thing that exalts itself against the word of God, and I bring every thought captive into the obedience of Christ.

Are you going to lead that thought away captive into the obedience of God's word, cast it down, reject it, or start speaking it and acting upon it?

Be not conformed to this world (this age) fashioned after and adapted to its external, superficial customs, but be transformed (changed) by the entire renewal of your mind (by the Word of God) so that you may prove what the good and acceptable and perfect will of God is. *(Romans 12:2)*

Your Word have I hidden in my heart so that I may not sin against thee. I must set my mind and keep it set on what is above (the higher things) not on the things that are on the earth.

What is my mind set on? You can have a determined mind set to stop doing that, or to start doing something that will change your life for the good or for the bad. Some people's minds are already made up and they do not want to be confused by the truth.

How do the evil thoughts (reasonings, debates, disputings and designs) get into the heart? They come in through what we see and hear which; in turn, affects your mind (your way of thinking). That's where vain imaginings come from.

Vain: Empty, no real value, worthless, futile, unsuccessful.

For example: Looking at pornography, magazines, TV, movies, etc. If you keep looking at it, then you are going to start thinking about it, and then acting upon it.

Also, the same is true with the music you listen to. My mind must be renewed by the Word of

God. I must start thinking as He thinks, because we have the mind of Christ and hold the thoughts, feelings and purposes of His heart.

For those who are according to the flesh and are controlled by its unholy desires set their minds on and pursue those things which gratify the flesh, but those who are according to the spirit and are controlled by the desires of the Spirit, set their minds on and seek those things which gratify the Holy Spirit. *(Romans 8:5)*

Remember: you have the mind of Christ and hold the thoughts, feelings and purposes of His heart. You hear the voice of the good Shepherd and the voice of a stranger you will not follow.

What you think is what you believe! Remember: As a man thinks in his heart so is he. If we don't change our thinking to line up with God's, we will reap the corruption that is in the world.

You can't stop the buzzard from flying over your head, but you can stop him from building a nest in your hair.

Some of you may be hearing this for the first time. You were never taught this in church. In fact, some people believe that the gifts of prophecy, healing, tongues, etc. died a long time ago. That is exactly what we are talking about.

They believe it, because that is what they were taught, and because they believe it, they do not operate in any of the gifts that Christ gave the church.

There was a centurion whose servant was lying at the house paralyzed and distressed with intense pains. And Jesus said, "I will come and restore him."

But the centurion replied to Him: "Lord, I am not worthy or fit to have you come under my roof; but only speak the word, and my servant boy will be cured."

When Jesus heard him, He marveled and said to those who followed Him. "I tell you truly, I have not found so much faith as this with anyone, even in Israel."

Then to the centurion, Jesus said: "Go; it shall be done for you as you have BELIEVED!" The centurion spoke what he believed in his heart.

If we change our thinking to line up with God's word, it will eventually come out of our mouth. *(Matthew 8:5-13)*

Two blind men followed Jesus. I wondered about two blind men following Jesus. How did they see to follow Him? Either they were not totally blind, or someone led the way for them.

When He reached the house and went in, the blind men came to Him, and Jesus said to them. "Do you BELIEVE that I am able to do this?" They said to Him: "Yes, Lord." Then He touched their eyes, saying: "According to your faith and trust and reliance on the power invested in Me, be it done to you." *(Matthew 9:27)*

Do you see how your thinking affects what you BELIEVE?

Truly I tell you, whoever says to this mountain, be lifted up and thrown into the sea and does not doubt at all, in his heart, but BELIEVES that what he says will take place, it will be done for him.

You are not going to do it. He is! *(Mark 11:23)*

Whatever you ask for in prayer, BELIEVE.

You see, I BELIEVE everything that I have written about and taught in this book. I have overcome the enemy and this is what I BELIEVE!

If you were healed by God as you read this book, or if you were healed by applying these truths of the Word of God, or you received revelation from this book, please e-mail me at RevPaula@email.com and let me know. I would greatly appreciate hearing from you.

Also, please visit my website at:

www.SarasotaSchoolofFaith.com

Paula Struble is available for ministry and teaching at your event or location by contacting her by email or phoning her at her office in Sarasota at 941-350-5028.

Rev. Paula A. Struble

Paula is a minister of worship, teacher and operates in the gift of healing. She also is a leader of dramatic dance ministries. As a result of her personal healing of a serious disease early in 2005, her ministry is primarily in the area of healing. Her testimony of her present day healing will encourage you and let you know that God is still doing what He promised and your healing is for today.

Three physicians diagnosed Paula with Graves Disease in 2003. Graves Disease is an immune disorder that attacks the thyroid gland, causing it to run too slow or too fast. Her manifestation was the high-speed variety: hyperthyroidism. For two years Paula took a drug and was prescribed natural organic formulas every day to keep the thyroid stable. She waited for God to fulfill His healing promise, but her faith had not grown to the place where her inner man understood that she was already healed and that Jesus wasn't going to take that scourging again.

Paula was completely restored to health, with no pills, no therapy, no radiation, no surgery. The shaking stopped, her strength returned, weight increased, and her pulse returned to normal. Paula will be telling you her story of completion, and ministering in a powerful way, with the presence of the Holy Spirit to whom she has come to be closely related.

Paula Struble is ordained by the National Conservative Christian Church (www.NCCChurch.org) and lives in Sarasota, with her husband, Dr. Don Struble.

CPSIA information can be obtained at www.ICGtesting.com
Printed in the USA
LVOW06s2305170813

348404LV00001B/2/P

9 781457 509407